FROM SEA to SHINING SEA

RHODE ISLAND

VAL HALLINAN

Consultants

MELISSA N. MATUSEVICH, PH.D.
Curriculum and Instruction Specialist
Blacksburg, Virginia

MEAGAN COSTELLO
Librarian
The Lincoln School
Providence, Rhode Island

CHILDREN'S PRESS®

AN IMPRINT OF SCHOLASTIC INC.

New York • Toronto • London • Auckland • Sydney • Mexico City
New Delhi • Hong Kong • Danbury, Connecticut

Rhode Island is in the northeastern part of the United States. It is bordered by Massachusetts, Connecticut, and the Atlantic Ocean.

The photograph on the front cover shows Bristol Harbor at sunset.

Project Editor: Meredith DeSousa
Art Director: Marie O'Neill
Photo Researcher: Marybeth Kavanagh
Design: Robin West, Ox and Company, Inc.
Page 6 map and recipe art: Susan Hunt Yule
All other maps: XNR Productions, Inc.
Recipe p. 65 courtesy of Ganondagan State Historic Site.

Library of Congress Cataloging-in-Publication Data

Hallinan, Val.
    Rhode Island / Val Hallinan.
      p. cm. – (From sea to shining sea)
    Summary: An introduction to the state of Rhode Island, describing its geography, history, government, people, economy, and more. Includes bibliographical references and index.
  ISBN 13: 978-0-531-20812-0
  ISBN 10: 0-531-20812-5
  1. Rhode Island—Juvenile literature. [1. Rhode Island.] I. Title. II. Series.

F79.3 .H35 2008
974.5—dc22

                                                    2002014293

TABLE of CONTENTS

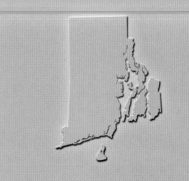

CHAPTER ONE

INTRODUCING THE OCEAN STATE

The Newport Harbor sparkles at dusk.

Rhode Island, a tiny area of land sometimes called "Little Rhody," is the smallest state in the nation. Despite its size, however, Rhode Island has played a big role in our country's history. As one of the original thirteen colonies, it contributed to the birth of the United States and the shaping of its government.

History tells us that the people of Rhode Island like to be first and they like to be different. In fact, when Rhode Island was still a colony of Great Britain, it became known as the place "where people think otherwise." A colony is part of a new country where a large group of people move who are still ruled by the leaders and laws of their old country. Rhode Island was the first of the American colonies to declare itself free from British rule, and the first to make it against the law to import enslaved Africans. It was also the first—and only—colony to welcome people of all religions.

Another important first came from Rhode Island, when Samuel Slater built the first water-powered mill for cloth making in the country there. This marked the beginning of the Industrial Revolution in the United States. Goods once made by hand could now be made more quickly and in greater numbers by machines. Eventually, Rhode Island became known for one industry in particular—jewelry.

Today, Rhode Island is also known for its scenic beauty. It is sometimes called the Ocean State because the Narragansett Bay, an arm of the Atlantic Ocean, almost cuts the state in half. The Ocean State's forty-one public saltwater and twenty-two freshwater beaches draw thousands of beach lovers each year.

What else comes to mind when you think of Rhode Island?

❖ Tourists taking the ferry to Block Island
❖ U.S. Navy ships sailing into Newport
❖ Jewelers and silversmiths making costume jewelry and silverware
❖ Music lovers dancing to the sweet sounds of the Newport Jazz Festival
❖ Some of the best sailors in the world competing in yacht races along the coast
❖ Scientists studying the ocean at the University of Rhode Island

Rhode Islanders haven't forgotten their rich and colorful past. They carefully preserve their state's many historical treasures for visitors to enjoy. Many of Newport's mansions, which once served as summer homes of the newly rich, have been lovingly restored. To learn more about this special state, simply turn the page. Welcome to Rhode Island!

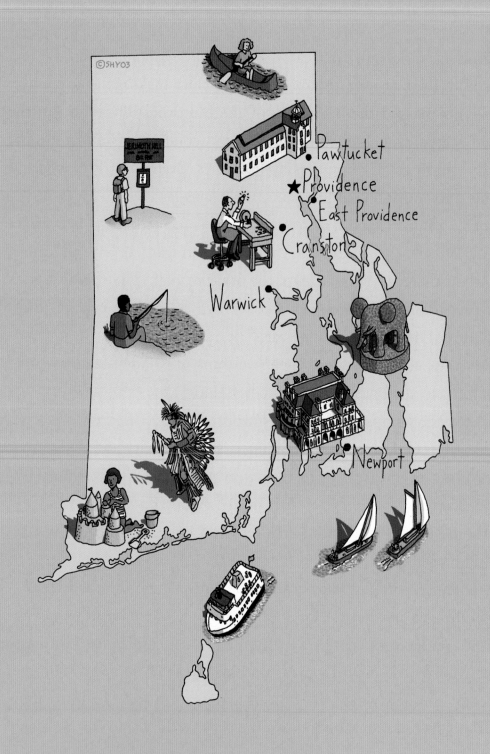

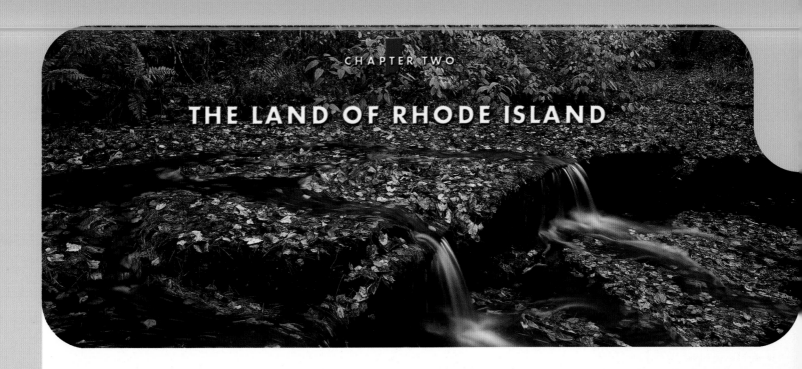

CHAPTER TWO

THE LAND OF RHODE ISLAND

Water tells the story of the Ocean State just as much as its land does. Rhode Island's history is filled with tales of shipwrecks and English schooners set afire by colonists fighting for freedom. Its beautiful coastline inspired some of the richest people in the world to build vacation homes there. It also provided the perfect setting for a lively shipbuilding industry.

The smallest of the fifty states, Rhode Island is only 48 miles (77 kilometers) from north to south and 37 miles (60 km) from east to west. It is in a region of the northeastern United States known as New England. The commonwealth of Massachusetts forms Rhode Island's northern and eastern borders. Connecticut is Rhode Island's neighbor to the west. The Atlantic Ocean is the state's southern border.

The Ocean State has thirty-six islands. Aquidneck Island is the largest. All of the islands except one are in Narragansett Bay, which is an arm of

The Arcadia Management Area in south central Rhode Island is a great place to enjoy the outdoors.

FIND OUT MORE

The University of Rhode Island's Graduate School of Oceanography is in Narragansett. It is one of the finest centers of oceanography (the study of oceans) in the country. Find out about studies scientists are doing that will help us take better care of our oceans and other bodies of water.

Block Island is a popular spot for vacationers.

the Atlantic Ocean that cuts Rhode Island nearly in half. Block Island lies just outside the bay in the Atlantic Ocean. Together, the state's seacoast, bays, and islands make up more than 400 miles (644 km) of coastline. No one in Rhode Island lives more than thirty minutes from the coast.

TWO LAND REGIONS

Thousands of years ago, glaciers, which are large masses of ice and snow, covered North America. As the glaciers moved and melted away, they left behind rocks, sand, gravel, and clay. The movements of the glaciers formed two land regions in Rhode Island: the Coastal Lowland and the New England Upland.

Coastal Lowland

The Coastal Lowland covers southern and eastern Rhode Island, almost two-thirds of the land in the state. Most of the mainland, the islands in Narragansett Bay, and the land that borders Massachusetts make up the Coastal Lowland. Rhode Island's largest cities are located within this region. Rhode Island's lowest point is at sea level in the lowland.

The shores of Rhode Island's lowland are lined with sandy beaches, salt ponds, marshes, and plains. The islands and the shore along Narragansett Bay have many beautiful, rocky cliffs. The Cliff Walk, a 3-mile (5-km) path along the ocean overlooking Rhode Island Sound in Newport, is a popular tourist attraction. Also, Block Island's Mohegan Bluffs offer a breathtaking vista, with ocean waves crashing below.

South County in the Coastal Lowland is best known for its seaside cottages, tidewater marshes, and ocean beaches.

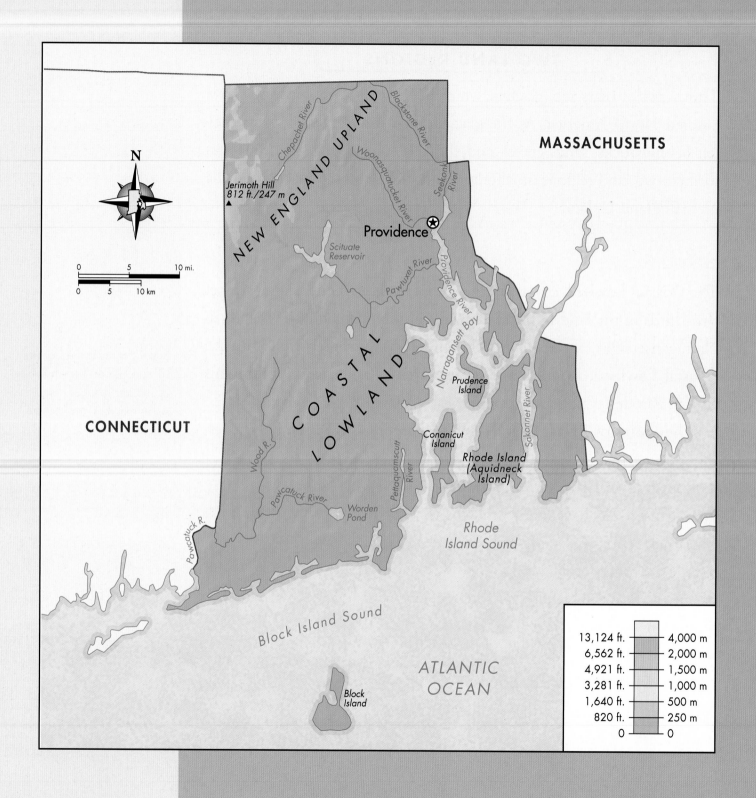

MASSACHUSETTS

CONNECTICUT

N

0   5   10 mi.
0   5   10 km

Chepachet River

Blackstone River

NEW ENGLAND UPLAND

Woonasquatucket River

Seekonk River

Jerimoth Hill
812 ft./247 m

Providence

Scituate
Reservoir

Pawtuxet River

Providence River

COASTAL
LOWLAND

Narragansett Bay

Prudence
Island

Wood R.

Conanicut
Island

Rhode Island
(Aquidneck
Island)

Sakonnet River

Pettaquamscutt River

Pawcatuck River

Worden
Pond

Pawcatuck R.

Rhode
Island Sound

Block Island Sound

ATLANTIC
OCEAN

Block
Island

13,124 ft.	4,000 m
6,562 ft.	2,000 m
4,921 ft.	1,500 m
3,281 ft.	1,000 m
1,640 ft.	500 m
820 ft.	250 m
0	0

Of all the state's islands, Aquidneck Island is the largest, with the towns of Newport, Middletown, and Portsmouth. There are also many tiny islands with names like Hog, Hen, Goat, and Gooseberry. The smallest is Despair Island, which is only a mound of rocks. In earlier days, there were many shipwrecks among the rocks in these dangerous waters.

Narragansett Bay has often been called the crown jewel of Rhode Island. Hundreds of thousands of tourists visit the bay every summer to enjoy swimming, boating, water skiing, and other activities. More than 3,800 commercial fishermen make a living fishing for shellfish, such as lobsters, crabs, oysters, and quahaugs, a type of clam, in the bay. They supply just under half of all the shellfish consumed in the United States.

An old lighthouse juts out of Narragansett Bay.

Over the years, pollution in the form of harmful industrial chemicals and waste material began to spoil this Ocean State treasure. Fish, shellfish, and other wildlife began to die out. An organization called Save the Bay, made up of people who want to keep Narragansett Bay clean, helped to pass laws against pollution. The water is cleaner now, and seals, dolphins, oysters, bluefish, striped bass, and squid are becoming plentiful again. However, billions of gallons of untreated sewage still flow into the bay. This is because sewer and stormwater pipes in Providence are very old. When there is heavy rain, overflow from sewage pipes is dumped into the bay. A plan is in place to update the system, but it will be expensive and take several years to build.

Another problem is that some of the bay has disappeared. About 4,000 acres (1,619 hectares) have been filled in so that offices and shops could be built there. Growth in Providence and the surrounding area is now being carefully planned so as not to endanger Narragansett Bay further.

New England Upland

Forests, rocky hills, and scattered farms make up the New England Upland in the northwestern part of the state. This region covers about one-third of Rhode Island, but it is less populated than the Coastal Lowland, which has the state's major cities and tourist attractions. The New England Upland has higher elevations than the Coastal Lowland. The highest point in the state, Jerimoth Hill in Foster, rises to 812 feet (247 meters).

The many sloping hills in the New England Upland shelter lakes, reservoirs, and ponds. The soil is thin and rocky, with few minerals. Christmas tree farms, nurseries that grow shrubs and turf (grass), and apple orchards dot the landscape. However, much of what was once farmland was returned to forest and woodlands because farming in the poor soil was so difficult for the early settlers. Among the upland's many trees, birches are especially plentiful. Much of Rhode Island's wildlife can be found in these forests and woodlands.

RIVERS AND LAKES

Rhode Island's rivers flow swiftly and have many waterfalls due to the rocky, uneven land. The energy of the rushing water powered the state's early mills and factories.

Three saltwater arms of the Narragansett Bay form the Providence, Sakonnet, and Seekonk rivers. The Pawtuxet, Pettaquamscutt, Potowomut, and Woonasquatucket are freshwater rivers that flow into Narragansett Bay. The Blackstone River begins in Massachusetts and becomes the Seekonk River before flowing into the bay. The first water-powered

Forests cover much of the New England Upland region.

13

mill in the country was built on the Blackstone River in 1790. Many mills along the Blackstone manufactured cotton thread and cloth, making Rhode Island an important center of industry. The Pawcatuck River forms Rhode Island's southwestern border with Connecticut, and is one of the few rivers in the state that does not flow into the bay.

There are nearly 300 lakes and ponds in Rhode Island. Humans made the largest inland body of water in the state, the Scituate Reservoir, by building a dam on the Pawtuxet River. Located in north central Rhode Island, the reservoir supplies water for Providence and other communities.

The Blackstone River is an important recreational and cultural resource in Rhode Island.

PLANT AND ANIMAL LIFE

Forests cover more than half of Rhode Island. Birches, cedars, hickories, maples, elms, oaks, and pines are among the trees that can be found in the state. Plants and flowers are also plentiful. Violets, mountain laurels, rhododendrons, and dogwoods grow in the forests. Freshwater and salt-water seaweed grow in Rhode Island waters.

Deer, foxes, muskrats, rabbits, raccoons, and squirrels make their home in the woodlands of Rhode Island, along with owls, catbirds, robins, and blue jays. Game birds include pheasants, wild ducks, and partridge. Terns, ospreys, cormorants, and gulls live on the coast. A number of sanctuaries there protect the nesting areas of the piping plover, a threatened species in Rhode Island.

Saltwater fish and shellfish are plentiful off the coast. Bluefish, butterfish, flounder, mackerel, bass, tuna, swordfish, lobsters, and clams live in the coastal waters. Freshwater fish in Rhode Island's rivers and lakes include trout, perch, bass, and pickerel.

Rabbits are among the many animals that live in Rhode Island.

CLIMATE

Rhode Island is blessed with a mild climate thanks to sea breezes that cool the land in summer and warm it in winter. The average temperature in July is 73° Fahrenheit (23° Celsius). In January, the average temperature is 28° F (–2° C). Average precipitation—rain, snow, and other forms of moisture—is 44 inches (112 centimeters). Most of the precipitation is snow, with an average of 31 inches (79 cm) per year. Snowfalls

are occasionally heavy, but they usually melt quickly.

The highest temperature ever recorded in Rhode Island was 104° F (40° C) on August 2, 1975, in Providence. Rhode Island's lowest recorded temperature was –25° F (–32° C) on February 5, 1996, at Greene.

FIND OUT MORE

Rhode Island has seen many fierce storms called hurricanes. These huge storms have strong, fast winds, heavy rain, and large ocean waves. The New England Hurricane of 1938 killed 262 Rhode Islanders. In 1991, Hurricane Bob caused $115 million in damage to the Ocean State. Find out about the latest advances in weather prediction that may help Rhode Island and other states better prepare for hurricanes.

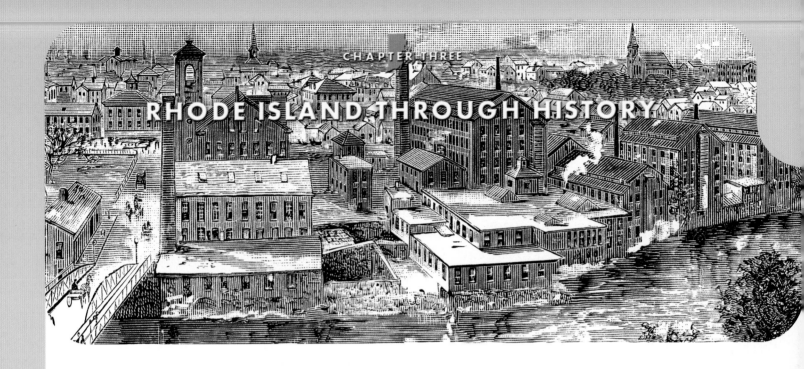

CHAPTER THREE

RHODE ISLAND THROUGH HISTORY

Archeologists study the life and culture of past peoples. They dig up the remains of structures and objects that give clues to what life was like long ago. Archeologists have found tools and weapons that indicate people lived in what is now Rhode Island as far back as 8,000 years ago. Because the continents of North America and Asia were attached long ago, scientists believe the early people of Rhode Island came from Asia. These early people hunted deer with spears made of stone and gathered clams along Narragansett Bay, but little else is known about their way of life.

Pawtucket was one of Rhode Island's most important industrial centers in the early 1800s.

FIND OUT MORE

What objects have archeologists discovered in your state that give clues to how people lived long ago? How did they discover these objects? Find out some of the scientific methods used to understand the clues left behind in the earth.

NATIVE AMERICANS

By the 1500s, about 8,000 Native Americans lived in the area that is now Rhode Island. They were divided into several tribes. Many belonged to the Algonquians, a large group of tribes related by language and customs. The Algonquians lived throughout the northeastern United States and eastern Canada.

The Narragansett was the largest of the Algonquian tribes in the Rhode Island area. They captured Aquidneck Island and land north of what is now the city of Providence from the Wampanoag, a tribe that lived to the east. The Narragansett fought the Pequot tribe as it tried to expand into Rhode Island from territory that is now Connecticut. They also took over the Cowesett and Shawomet tribes around 1630. The Nipmuck lived in the upper northwestern part of Rhode Island, and the Niantic lived along the southern coast.

The Narragansett lived in longhouses, which are long, narrow houses framed with logs and covered with bark. Women took care of the children and planted and harvested corn, squash, and beans. They also prepared food and made tools. The men fished and hunted.

EARLY EXPLORERS

Some historians and archeologists believe the Vikings were the first Europeans to come to Rhode Island. They know for sure that Giovanni da Verrazzano, an Italian working for France, sailed past what is now Rhode Island in 1524. He was searching for a water route through North America to China. Verrazzano never achieved his goal, but he wrote in his diary that he "discovered an island in the form of a triangle, distant from the mainland. . . about the bigness of the Island of Rhodes." Verrazzano was referring to the Greek island of Rhodes in the Aegean Sea. This may have been how Rhode Island got its name. The island he saw is called Block Island today.

Verrazzano and his crew made friends with the Wampanoag, who had rowed out to meet them. They guided Verrazzano to what is now Newport harbor. He spent two weeks there exploring the land and writing about the customs of the Wampanoag.

Almost one hundred years went by before the next European explorer visited Rhode Island. Dutch navigator Adriaen Block sailed past Block Island in 1614 on the way to the Hudson River. Block Island is named after him. Some people believe he also gave Rhode Island its name. He called it *Roodt Eylandt,* which means "red island" in Dutch, because of the red clay soil throughout the region.

Giovanni da Verrazzano was an Italian navigator who explored the East Coast of North America.

THE COLONIAL ERA

William Blackstone was the first European to settle in Rhode Island. He was a minister from England who broke away from the Church of England. At first, he settled on land that is now in Massachusetts. In 1635, he moved to what is now Rhode Island and built a home on the

Blackstone River, which was later named after him. Blackstone was a solitary man who lived by himself. The place where he settled belonged to Massachusetts until 1747, when it became part of Rhode Island.

In 1636, an English minister named Roger Williams created the first permanent settlement there. He would become known as the founder of Rhode Island. Williams had moved to Boston, Massachusetts, from England because he wanted to worship as he pleased rather than follow the Church of England. He lived in Massachusetts with his wife and children for five years working as a preacher and making friends with the Native Americans. Williams was very interested in Native Americans and their way of life, and he visited them often. He believed the English settlers were cheating Native Americans out of their land. He thought it was wrong to force Native Americans to convert to Christianity. Williams also thought that Christians should be free to choose how to worship God, and felt that church officials shouldn't be allowed to enforce laws. After he accused King James I of blasphemy (insulting God), he became an even bigger threat to the Puritan government.

The Puritans ordered Williams to leave Massachusetts, so in 1636 he obtained land from the Narragansett. Some historians believe Williams bought the land, but in his journal Williams wrote that he was given the land as a gift: ". . . not a penny was demanded . . . It was not price nor

money that could have purchased Rhode Island. Rhode Island was purchased by love."

In 1636, Williams and a small group of followers built the first non-Native American town in Rhode Island. Williams called the town Providence because the word refers to God's guidance and care. Providence was the first town in the country to allow total freedom of religion.

Within a few years, more settlements of people seeking religious freedom sprang up, including Portsmouth, Newport, Warwick, Wickford, and Pawtuxet. A very religious woman named Anne Hutchinson established modern-day Portsmouth after she was told to leave the Massachusetts Bay colony because of her religious views.

Anne Hutchinson (c. 1591–1643) was born in England and moved with her husband and children to the Massachusetts Bay Colony in search of religious freedom. However, the Puritans there did not agree with Hutchinson's beliefs, and they did not allow women to preach. The Puritans banished her from Massachusetts as "a woman unfit for society." Anne fled to Rhode Island and helped to found Pocasset (now Portsmouth) in 1638, where she continued to preach and practice her faith.

In 1644, Great Britain granted a charter, or written statement of rights, allowing Roger Williams to unite Providence, Newport, Warwick, and Portsmouth into a colony known as the Providence Plantations. The four settlements were officially united in 1647. Several years later, in 1663, King Charles II of England granted a new charter to the tiny colony. It allowed the colony to govern itself and permitted total freedom of religion. The charter said the colony of Rhode Island was "a lively experiment . . . with full liberty in religious commitments." Rhode Island had become the first democracy in the New World. A democracy is a form of government in which people govern themselves through elected representatives. The official name, "Rhode Island and Providence Plantations," was adopted in this charter. The Charter of 1663 served as the foundation of Rhode Island for nearly 200 years.

Throughout the 1600s, Rhode Island welcomed people of many faiths. In 1639, a group of Christians known as Baptists established a church in Providence, their first in the United States. Another branch of Christianity, the Quakers, built a meetinghouse on Aquidneck Island in 1657. Newport welcomed a group of Jewish believers in 1658. They built their first synagogue, or place of worship, in the

United States in Newport. A group of French Calvinists, another branch of Christianity, settled in East Greenwich in 1686.

LIFE IN THE EARLY DAYS

Even though Rhode Island had the greatest variety of religions, it had the smallest population of all the colonies. In 1660, there were 20,000 people in the Massachusetts Bay colony, 8,500 in the Maryland colony, 2,000 in the Plymouth colony, and only about 1,500 in Rhode Island.

The Baptist Church in Providence was one of many houses of worship in Rhode Island during the 1600s.

Throughout the 1600s, settlers in the British colonies earned a living by farming. Most Rhode Islanders lived on small farms and raised their own crops and livestock. At first, these early settlers lived in dugouts carved into hillsides and crude huts made of saplings, bark, and fur. Later, they built one-room dwellings of wood with thatch or sod roofs. Large fireplaces with ovens were used for cooking and heating the homes.

Rhode Islanders grew corn, peas, and oats and raised hogs, goats, cattle, sheep, and horses. A few families owned larger farms and grew wealthy by selling butter, cheese, beef, pork, mutton, and wool to other colonies. To help run the farms, some wealthy families owned more than one hundred enslaved Africans, who were brought to the colonies against their will to work in the fields and help with household chores. These Africans were not treated like human beings. They were bought and sold as if they were goods. Often, African families were split up and sold to different owners. Slaves were given food and lodging, but they were not paid for their work.

KING PHILIP'S WAR

While the colonists in New England prospered, Native Americans suffered. Many died from diseases brought by unsuspecting European settlers. Colonists also took Native American land. The two cultures were very different in their beliefs and lifestyles and they often fought with one another.

In 1675, the Narragansett and other tribes decided to drive the colonists out of New England. Led by Metacomet, a Wampanoag chief also known as King Philip, Native Americans began attacking colonial settlements. Most of the battles of King Philip's War (1675–1676) were fought in Massachusetts, but one major battle known as the Great Swamp Fight took place in Rhode Island. On December 19, 1675, an army of 1,000 colonists attacked and set fire to a large Narragansett village near what is now West Kingston. By the time the fighting was over, about 350 Native American men, women, and children had been slain

The colonists launched a surprise attack on the Narragansett in December 1675.

or burned to death. It was one of the largest killings of Native Americans in American history.

In the late summer of 1676, an army of colonists and Native Americans who were against King Philip captured nearly 200 Native Americans in Massachusetts. King Philip's wife and son were captured, but Philip fled to Rhode Island. On August 12, he was ambushed and killed by a Native American who was friendly with the colonial side. The war ended soon after, and several thousand Native Americans had been killed. The Wampanoag and Narragansett tribes were nearly wiped out.

By 1682, fewer than 500 Narragansett lived in Rhode Island. Eventually, the small tribes that remained formed a new Narragansett community in Charlestown, which is still active today.

WHO'S WHO IN RHODE ISLAND?

Metacomet (c. 1638–1676) was a Wampanoag chief called King Philip by the colonists. His father, Massasoit, gave land to Roger Williams. In King Philip's War, Metacomet fought unsuccessfully to get back his people's land. Metacomet was born near present-day Bristol.

THE TRIANGLE TRADE

During its early days, Rhode Island imported more enslaved Africans than any other colony. A trade route with three points developed and became known as the Triangle Trade. The three points were Newport, Africa, and the West Indies. Merchants from Newport imported molasses from the West Indies and made it into rum. Then the Newport merchants shipped the rum to Africa and traded it to slavers. Many of the enslaved Africans were brought to the West Indies and traded for molasses. Some enslaved Africans were also sold to landholders with vast cotton and tobacco plantations (farms) in the South and to farmers with lots of land in Rhode Island. The landholders used the enslaved Africans as farmworkers and servants.

During the 1730s, commercial activity flourished in the Newport area.

Conditions on board the slave ships from Africa were crowded and dirty. Enslaved Africans were packed into small quarters below deck. Many died from disease or starvation. The Brown brothers of Providence—Nicholas, Moses, John, and Joseph—were wealthy merchants who bought and sold Africans. Although the Brown family did many good things for Providence, such as building churches and schools, a great deal of the money they made came from the profits of trading enslaved Africans and making rum. Eventually, Moses Brown realized the evils of slavery and worked to end the slave trade. In 1784, Rhode Island passed the Negro Emancipation Act, which provided for the gradual emancipation, or freeing, of the children of enslaved Africans when the men turned twenty-one and the women eighteen.

THE REVOLUTIONARY WAR

By the mid 1700s, settlers from Great Britain had established thirteen colonies along the East Coast of what is now the United States. But relations between Great Britain and its colonies were unfriendly. The colonies did not want to be ruled by a country far across the Atlantic Ocean. They wanted to govern themselves. Great Britain had passed many laws that limited how much the colonies could trade with other countries. The colonies often ignored these laws and smuggled, or transported in secret, goods from other countries into ports on the East Coast. Beginning in 1764, Britain made the colonists pay high taxes (fees) on goods they imported from Britain, such as sugar, tea, and

WHO'S WHO IN RHODE ISLAND?

Nicholas Brown (1729–1791) was one of four brothers in Providence's leading merchant family. He helped found Rhode Island College, later renamed Brown University in his honor. Nicholas Brown also helped to convince Rhode Islanders to approve the United States Constitution.

The burning of the *Gaspee*, a British ship, was one of the most famous acts of colonial defiance.

paper. These taxes made the colonists very angry. To protest, they made straw dummies that represented British tax collectors and burned them.

True to its free spirit, Rhode Island did not hesitate to protest the English laws. Rhode Islanders had always enjoyed more freedom than the other colonies, thanks to their unique charter granted by King Charles II in 1663. Rhode Islanders were not about to stand for having their freedom taken away. In 1769, angry Rhode Islanders burned the English ship *Liberty* in Newport. In 1772, they set fire to the *Gaspee* near Providence. The burning of the *Liberty* and *Gaspee* were just two of many acts of rebellion against Britain that occurred in the colonies.

The American Revolution (1775–1783) began in Massachusetts at the Battle of Lexington on April 19, 1775. British soldiers had been sent to capture American leaders and seize some gunpowder. They were met with about 75 colonists who were armed. A shot was fired, but no one knows which side fired the shot. The British then began shooting. They killed eight colonists and wounded ten others.

There were more battles. One by one, the colonies declared independence from Great Britain. Rhode Island led the way by becoming the first colony to declare its freedom on May 4, 1776. On July 4, 1776, representatives from all the colonies approved a Declaration of Independence stating that the colonies were "free and independent states." Two Rhode Islanders, Stephen Hopkins and William Ellery, were members of this group of representatives called the Congress. They signed the Declaration of Independence along with the other members of Congress.

Many Rhode Islanders fought in the American Revolution. Two brothers, Stephen and Esek Hopkins, helped form the colonial navy, known as the Continental Navy. Rhode Islander General Nathanael Greene was second-in-command to General George Washington, who led the Continental Army, made up of soldiers from all of the colonies.

The most important fighting of the American Revolution in Rhode Island was the Battle of Rhode Island on August 29, 1778. The Continental Army wanted to capture Newport, which was being held by the British. General John Sullivan planned to lead the attack on Newport. He was counting on help from the French, who had entered the war on the American side. However, the vessels carrying French troops were destroyed in a storm in Narragansett Bay, so Sullivan and his troops decided to retreat to Portsmouth, where they met other British troops and engaged in battle.

Nathanael Greene was one of the most revered generals of the Continental army.

In the Battle of Rhode Island, American colonists successfully escaped from Newport without capture by the British.

Although the British lost more men in this battle than the Continental Army, Sullivan was still not able to win back Newport without help from the French, so he retreated from Rhode Island.

The first African-American army unit in history, the Black Regiment of Rhode Island, fought in the Battle of Rhode Island and many other Revolutionary War battles. The French General Marquis de Lafayette described the Black Regiment's actions in the Battle of Rhode Island as the "best fought action of the war."

General Nathanael Greene helped set in motion the final British defeat in the American Revolution. Greene led American troops in the South and forced the British to retreat out of the Carolinas and into Yorktown, Virginia, in 1781. General George Washington was then able to attack Yorktown, where the British surrendered. The thirteen

colonies had won the Revolutionary War. They signed a peace treaty with the British in September 1783.

At first, the newly formed country was governed by a document known as the Articles of Confederation. This document stated the laws of the new country. It gave the former colonies, now known as states, a lot of power and created a weak central government. Finally freed from British rule, people did not want a strong government to have control over their lives. Many felt more loyalty to their state than to their new country.

A weak central government created many problems, however. There was no president to lead the country. The government was not allowed to collect taxes, and so it had no money. Some states did not get along, and the central government was too weak to settle disputes. However, many people remained opposed to a strong central government. Most Rhode Islanders were against it because they thought the larger states would have more power than the smaller states. They did not want the government to interfere with shipping and trading. When a national convention was held in Philadelphia in 1787, Rhode Island did not send representatives.

A new governing document was written at the convention. The Constitution explained the laws and principles that would govern the United States. Nine states had to approve the Constitution before it could go into effect. New Hampshire was the ninth state to approve the Constitution, on June 21, 1788. Eventually, every state had approved it, except for Rhode Island.

When a Bill of Rights was added to the Constitution, more Rhode Islanders were in favor of approving it. The Bill of Rights limited the power of the government by guaranteeing basic rights and freedoms to all. On May 29, 1790, Rhode Island approved the United States Constitution by a vote of 34 to 32.

BIRTHPLACE OF THE AMERICAN INDUSTRIAL REVOLUTION

Rhode Island became a leader in industry after the Revolutionary War. Along the banks of the Blackstone River at Pawtucket, a businessman from England named Samuel Slater built the country's first water-powered mill. A mill is a building or group of buildings used to manufacture goods, such as textiles (cloth). Slater captured the power of the waterfalls to make cotton yarn faster than ever before. The flowing water of the Blackstone River turned a very large waterwheel and a series of gears connected to the wheel. These gears powered machinery that spun cotton into thread.

Slater's Mill became known as the birthplace of the American Industrial Revolution. The Industrial Revolution changed the way people lived. Instead of making goods by hand, workers used water-powered machines and power tools to make goods. Machines could run all the time and manufacture goods much faster than humans alone. More goods were available than ever before, and jobs were plentiful. Many people left farming and moved to industrial centers where there were jobs in manufacturing.

The new textile mills employed many people, including men, women, and children.

This illustration shows Pawtucket Falls in the 1790s. At that time the falls powered many textile mills in the area.

After Slater's Mill opened, many other factories sprang up in Pawtucket. These factories produced tools, gears, spinning wheels, and other goods. Factory jobs attracted many people, and Pawtucket grew rapidly, becoming a center of industry.

In 1794, businessmen Nehemiah and Seril Dodge of Providence opened a jewelry-making business. Providence soon had more factories than any other city in New England. Meanwhile, silversmith Jabez Gorham began producing sterling silver. Whaling and fishing also became important industries. Whale oil was used to make can-

FIND OUT MORE

Samuel Slater's water-powered mill helped launch the Industrial Revolution, which dramatically changed the way people live and work. What twentieth century inventions had a great impact on our society? What new inventions do you think will come along in the twenty-first century to change our lives?

dles and other products. The nearby cities of Boston and New York were huge markets for Rhode Island's flourishing industries.

WAR AND PROSPERITY

In 1812, the United States once again went to war with Britain. The two countries fought over ownership of land in the west and other issues. Two heroes from Rhode Island helped the United States win the war: Oliver Hazard Perry and his brother, Matthew Calbraith Perry. Oliver Perry commanded the fleet of ships that won the Battle of Lake Erie. He sent a message to General William Henry Harrison that became famous: "We have met the enemy and they are ours." Matthew Perry served in the U.S. Navy during the War of 1812 and later opened up trade between Japan and the United States.

Meanwhile, people from Ireland, Sweden, Germany, Portugal, southern and eastern Europe, and Canada had begun pouring in to Rhode Island to work in the many factories and mills. These newcomers, or immigrants, helped double the state's population during the first half of the nineteenth century. Between 1800 and 1850, Rhode Island's population rose from 69,122 to 147,545.

People realized Rhode Island needed new laws now that the state had many growing cities. The state was still governed by the charter of 1663,

Oliver Hazard Perry became famous for his role in the War of 1812.

FAMOUS FIRSTS

- In 1824, women weavers of Pawtucket went on strike and refused to work until their demands for higher pay and better working conditions were met. Their strike is thought to be the first one in the United States by women.
- In 1866, the country's first public roller skating rink opened in Newport.
- In 1896, the country's first auto race on a track was held in Cranston. The cars traveled about 25 miles (40 km) per hour.
- In 1960, the first fully mechanized post office in the United States opened in Providence.

Thomas Dorr (above) and his followers, called "Dorrites," tried to reform, or change, Rhode Island's government.

which allowed only landowners and their eldest sons to vote. This meant most people who lived in the cities could not vote in state elections.

Thomas Dorr, a lawyer from Providence, led a call for reform (change) that became known as the Dorr Rebellion. He wanted to form a new state government. Dorr failed, but Rhode Island adopted a new constitution shortly thereafter. It went into effect in 1843 and is still used today. The new constitution gave voting rights to more people, although women were still denied the right to vote. It gave native-born males, including African Americans, the right to vote if they met a three-year residency requirement. Women could not vote in Rhode Island until 1917.

THE WAR BETWEEN THE STATES

In 1861, civil war split the United States. The war between the northern states and southern states erupted over slavery and other issues. Slavery had been outlawed in Rhode Island in 1784, and by 1820 it was against the law in other northern states. A network of people who wanted to end slavery formed what became known as the Underground Railroad.

"Conductors" of the Underground Railroad secretly helped enslaved Africans get from one safe house to another.

This secret network of people and hiding places was created to help enslaved Africans escape to freedom in Canada. Some Rhode Islanders took part in the Underground Railroad. Elizabeth Buffum Chace hid runaway slaves at her home in Central Falls. Moses Brown, once an importer of slaves and a member of a wealthy family of merchants in Providence, supported the Underground Railroad.

The southern states wanted to break away and form their own government so they could be free to enslave Africans. Together, they formed a new nation called the Confederate States of America. Many Rhode Islanders

WHO'S WHO IN RHODE ISLAND?

Elizabeth Buffum Chace (1806–1899) fought for women's rights and an end to slavery. She and her husband hid enslaved Africans in their Central Falls home. Chace also worked for better conditions for women prisoners, helped found a school for homeless children, and fought for Brown University to admit women. She resigned from the Providence Women's Club in 1876 because it refused to admit an African American schoolteacher.

did not want to fight against the Confederate Army. Rhode Island was the center of the textile industry, and enslaved Africans working in the South produced the cotton from which fabric and thread were made. However, other Rhode Islanders supported going to war because they felt that the United States was stronger as one unified nation.

Even though Rhode Islanders didn't agree on many of the issues dividing the North and the South, more than 24,000 of them volunteered to serve in the Navy and the Union Army (the army of the northern states) during the Civil War (1861–1865). About 2,000 of these volunteers were African-American. Major General Ambrose E. Burnside commanded the Army of the Potomac for part of the war. He later became governor of Rhode Island and a United States senator.

Rhode Island also produced war materials such as rifles, bayonets, uniforms, blankets, and tents. By the time the Civil War ended in victory for the North in 1865, Rhode Island had become a much wealthier state.

Onlookers in Knoxville, Tennessee, welcomed General Burnside and his troops from Rhode Island.

(opposite) Vacationers have long enjoyed the beauty of Rhode Island's coast.

A GROWING STATE

Always a center of naval activities, Rhode Island became the home of the Newport Naval Station in 1883. The following year the Naval War College opened in Newport. It became the country's leading center for naval training and education. By this time, Newport had also become a popular vacation spot for some of the wealthiest people in the country. Many beautiful and lavish mansions sprang up along Bellevue Avenue and Ocean Drive, and the rich people who lived there helped Newport become a center of arts and culture.

By the end of the century, more than 1,500 factories in Rhode Island were producing many kinds of goods, including textiles, machinery, silver, and jewelry. Between 1900 and 1910, the state's population increased from 429,000 to 543,000 as immigrants sought work in the many factories. Italians, Russians, Germans, French, Poles, Armenians, Lithuanians, and Ukrainians became a part of Rhode Island's culture, as did their traditions and customs.

THE TWENTIETH CENTURY

A new century brought two world wars and many ups and downs for Rhode Island. During World War I (1914–1918), the United States, Great Britain, France, and other countries fought against Germany and Austria-Hungary. Many Rhode Islanders fought and died in World War I. The state produced ammunition, combat ships, and chemicals that helped the war effort.

Once World War I ended, Rhode Island began to lose jobs. Textile manufacturers began to move to the southern states because it was cheaper to do business there. Wages and taxes were lower in the South, and manufacturers did not have to pay to have cotton shipped to the North.

To make matters worse, the Great Depression (1929–1939) severely weakened business and industry in the United States and Europe. A depression is when business slows down and many people lose their jobs. The New York Stock Exchange crash of 1929 marked the beginning of the Great Depression. The Stock Exchange is where shares of companies and businesses are bought and sold. These shares are known as stocks. During the late 1920s, stocks had become very expensive. But people began to realize these stocks were not really worth that much money. Many stock owners began selling their stocks, and stock prices tumbled. People and businesses whose stocks had been worth millions of dollars now had stocks worth only pennies.

During the Great Depression, soup kitchens provided free meals for many Americans.

Many businesses, factories, and banks closed, because they had used their money to buy stocks. People who had money in those banks lost all of their savings. In Rhode Island, thousands of people lost their jobs, because factories could not afford to pay workers. In 1923, 34,000 Rhode Islanders worked in textile mills. By 1938, the number of Rhode Islanders working in textile mills had dropped to 12,000.

One in four Americans could not find work. In Rhode Island and across the country, it was common to see people standing in long lines known as breadlines, waiting for free bread, coffee, and soup from charities. Some people lived in the streets and searched for food in garbage dumps.

When Franklin D. Roosevelt was elected president of the United States, he worked to end the Great Depression. He started a government program called the New Deal, which helped create jobs. The Civilian Conservation Corps (CCC) was an important part of the New Deal. It placed people in jobs such as cleaning up national parks and planting trees. The Works Progress Administration (WPA), another New Deal program, put people to work on projects to benefit the public. Providence and other Rhode Island cities gave people jobs constructing roads, improving parks, and building schools and public buildings.

Business and manufacturing did not really recover from the Great Depression until world war erupted again. During World War II (1939–1945), the United States, Great Britain, and other countries fought against Germany, Italy, and Japan. Factories became busy again manufacturing war supplies. People who had been out of work for a long time had jobs again.

About 100,000 Rhode Islanders served in World War II. While soldiers fought overseas, Rhode Island industry geared up to help the war effort. A torpedo factory on Goat Island made almost 8 in 10 torpedoes used in World War II. In 1941, the U.S. Navy opened the Quonset Point Naval Air Station in Rhode Island. Many people found jobs there

A platoon of American troops stands in formation in front of a row of quonset huts.

building quonset huts, a new kind of war shelter made of sheet metal. Quonset huts were used as sleeping quarters, hospitals, churches, and storage rooms.

After the war, Rhode Island once again saw hard times. By 1949, many Rhode Islanders were out of work because much of the textile industry had moved to the South where costs were lower. Fortunately, new industries sprang up during the 1950s and 1960s. Electronics, chemicals, machinery, and plastics manufacturing meant new jobs and a stronger economy. New roads and freeways opened up Rhode Island to tourists, creating more jobs.

WHAT'S IN A NAME?

The names of many Rhode Island places have interesting origins.

Name	Comes From or Means
Narragansett	The English mistakenly referred to the Native Americans in Rhode Island as *Narragansett*, instead of *Nanhigganeuck*, which means "people of the small point"
Providence	A word used by the Puritans that means "God's watchful care"
Pawtucket River	Algonquian word for "place of rushing water"

MODERN TIMES

In 1973, President Richard Nixon took much of the naval fleet out of Newport. This put about 21,000 Rhode Islanders who had jobs related to the military out of work. Much of the land that belonged to the Navy was given to the state for public recreation. Even though Rhode Island lost jobs, it gained land that was turned into the Bay Island Park System, which many Rhode Islanders enjoy today.

In 1991, Rhode Island suffered a banking crisis, partly because of dishonest practices in business and government. About forty-five state-chartered banks and credit unions closed. One in five Rhode Islanders couldn't get their savings out of the bank. Many people couldn't make their house or car payments. Eventually, people got their money back, but sometimes it took as long as three years.

Despite some difficult times in recent years, Rhode Islanders have bounced back. The state's future is bright. It remains the jewelry capital of the world. Several corporations have headquarters in Rhode Island. Despite the loss of the naval air station, industries such as Electric Boat, which makes sections of submarines, and Toray Plastics (America) provide employment to thousands of Rhode Islanders. Electronics and other high-technology fields offer many jobs that pay well. Rhode Island's tourist attractions also bring many visitors—and dollars—into the state. More people than ever are discovering what a great place the smallest state is.

Newport is a popular place for tourists in Rhode Island.

CHAPTER FOUR

GOVERNING RHODE ISLAND

The government of Rhode Island centers around the State House in Providence.

Rhode Island's constitution, a document listing the basic laws of the state, was adopted in 1843. It was created shortly after the Dorr Rebellion. Thomas Dorr wanted people to have a greater voice in government. His followers wrote a People's Constitution and elected Dorr as governor, but the constitution was not valid. Instead, a new constitution was written that had some of Dorr's ideas. For example, it said that adult males—including African Americans—didn't have to own property in order to vote, but they had to be born in the United States. Male citizens born in another country had to own property in Rhode Island to vote.

Rhode Island's constitution includes more than forty amendments, or changes. The constitution can be changed only if a majority of the legislature (the law-making branch of the government) agrees, followed by a majority vote of the citizens.

Rhode Island's government is made up of three branches, or parts. The legislative branch creates the laws. The executive branch enforces the laws. The judicial branch interprets, or explains, the laws.

LEGISLATIVE BRANCH

Rhode Island's legislative branch, or legislature, is called the General Assembly. It consists of a senate made up of thirty-eight members and a house of representatives made up of seventy-five members. Members of the General Assembly are elected by voters to serve two-year terms. General Assembly sessions begin on the first Tuesday of every January and last for at least sixty working days, sometimes longer. The General Assembly may also call special sessions.

The state legislature makes laws that govern Rhode Islanders. For example, in 1951 the legislature gave home rule to Rhode Island's cities and towns. This means they are allowed to write their own charters. The charter of a city or town states how the government is organized and outlines its powers.

A proposed new law is called a bill. After the legislature votes in favor of a bill, the governor of Rhode Island must either approve or veto (reject) it. If the governor vetoes the bill, the legislature may overrule the veto if at least three-fifths of the members vote to do so.

Members of the Rhode Island State Senate meet inside the capitol to discuss new laws.

The legislature also has the power to amend, or change, the state constitution. If an amendment is proposed in the state legislature, it must be approved by the majority of legislators and then voted on by the citizens of Rhode Island. Three-fifths of voters must approve the amendment for it to become a law.

EXECUTIVE BRANCH

The governor is head of the executive branch. He or she is elected to a four-year term and may serve no more than eight years. The lieutenant governor, secretary of state, attorney general, and general treasurer are also part of the executive branch. Each of these positions is elected to serve for four years. With the approval of the state senate, the governor appoints the heads of government departments. These departments include environment, health, labor, and transportation.

JUDICIAL BRANCH

The court system is responsible for interpreting, or explaining, the laws of the state. There are different levels of courts. The head of Rhode Island's judicial branch is the supreme court. A chief justice (judge) and four associate justices are elected by the General Assembly to serve on

RHODE ISLAND GOVERNORS

Name	Term	Name	Term
Nicholas Cooke	1775–1778	John W. Davis	1887–1888
William Greene	1778–1786	Royal C. Taft	1888–1889
John Collins	1786–1790	Herbert W. Ladd	1889–1890
Arthur Fenner	1790–1805	John W. Davis	1890–1891
Henry Smith	1805	Herbert W. Ladd	1891–1892
Isaac Wilbur	1806–1807	D. Russell Brown	1892–1895
James Fenner	1807–1811	Charles W. Lippitt	1895–1897
William Jones	1811–1817	Elisha Dyer	1897–1900
Nehemiah R. Knight	1817–1821	William Gregory	1900–1901
William C. Gibbs	1821–1824	Charles D. Kimball	1901–1903
James Fenner	1824–1831	Lucius F. C. Garvin	1903–1905
Lemuel H. Arnold	1831–1833	George H. Utter	1905–1907
John Brown Francis	1833–1838	James H. Higgins	1907–1909
William Sprague	1838–1839	Aram J. Pothier	1909–1915
Samuel Ward King	1840–1843	R. Livingston Beeckman	1915–1921
James Fenner	1843–1845	Emery J. San Souci	1921–1923
Charles Jackson	1845–1846	William S. Flynn	1923–1925
Byron Diman	1846–1847	Aram J. Pothier	1925–1928
Elisha Harris	1847–1849	Norman S. Case	1928–1933
Henry B. Anthony	1849–1851	Theodore F. Green	1933–1937
Philip Allen	1851–1853	Robert E. Quinn	1937–1939
Francis M. Dimond	1853–1854	William H. Vanderbilt	1939–1941
William W. Hoppin	1854–1857	J. Howard McGrath	1941–1945
Elisha Dyer	1857–1859	John O. Pastore	1945–1950
Thomas G. Turner	1859–1860	John S. McKiernan	1950–1951
William Sprague	1860–1863	Dennis J. Roberts	1951–1959
William C. Cozzens	1863	Christopher Del Sesto	1959–1961
James Y. Smith	1863–1866	John A. Notte, Jr.	1961–1963
Ambrose E. Burnside	1866–1869	John H. Chafee	1963–1969
Seth Padelford	1869–1873	Frank Licht	1969–1973
Henry Howard	1873–1875	Philip W. Noel	1973–1977
Henry Lippitt	1875–1877	J. Joseph Garrahy	1977–1985
Charles C. Van Zandt	1877–1880	Edward D. DiPrete	1985–1991
Alfred H. Littlefield	1880–1883	Bruce G. Sundlun	1991–1995
Augustus O. Bourn	1883–1885	Lincoln C. Almond	1995–2003
George P. Wetmore	1885–1887	Donald L. Carcieri	2003–

RHODE ISLAND STATE GOVERNMENT

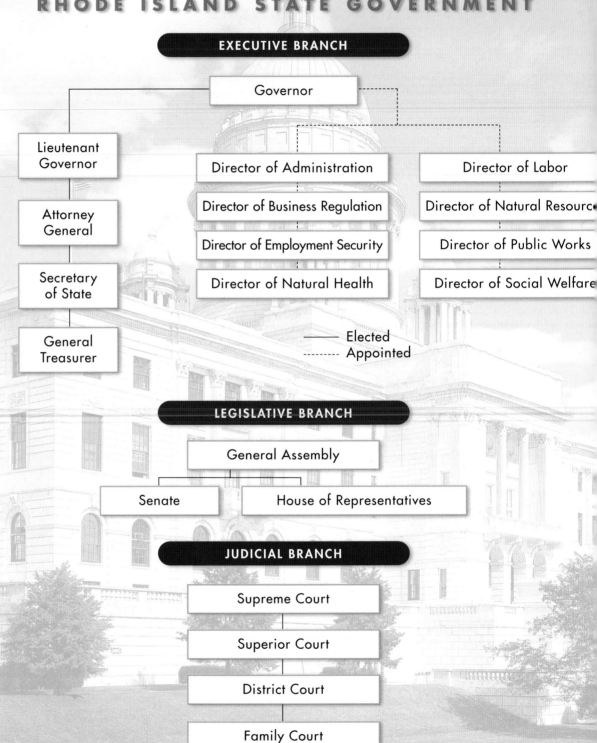

EXECUTIVE BRANCH

Governor

Lieutenant Governor

Attorney General

Secretary of State

General Treasurer

Director of Administration

Director of Business Regulation

Director of Employment Security

Director of Natural Health

Director of Labor

Director of Natural Resources

Director of Public Works

Director of Social Welfare

—— Elected
------ Appointed

LEGISLATIVE BRANCH

General Assembly

Senate

House of Representatives

JUDICIAL BRANCH

Supreme Court

Superior Court

District Court

Family Court

the supreme court for life. The supreme court rules over all the lower courts. If a person does not agree with the decision of a lower court, he or she may request a review of their case by the state supreme court.

Among the lower courts, the superior court has twenty-one associate justices and one presiding judge. This court hears criminal cases—those in which someone is accused of breaking a law—and civil cases involving property valued at more than $5,000. (A civil case is one in which two or more parties disagree about the meaning of a law.)

Other courts in Rhode Island include district courts, a traffic tribunal, a workers' compensation court, and family court. District courts hear cases involving misdemeanors (minor crimes) and small claims. Cases brought to family court involve decisions about divorce, adoption, and other family matters. The workers' compensation court hears disputes between an injured employee and his or her employer, and the traffic tribunal handles cases involving traffic violations, such as reckless driving.

LOCAL GOVERNMENT

Rhode Island has five counties: Providence, Kent, Washington, Bristol, and Newport. It is one of only two states with no county governments. (Connecticut is the other state.)

Rhode Island has eight cities and thirty-one towns. Of these, seven cities and twenty-five towns have home rule. Most of Rhode Island's large cities have a mayor and a city council. A city council is a group of elected members who make the city laws. These include Providence, Newport, Warwick, Pawtucket, and Woonsocket. East Providence and Middletown have a city council and a city manager.

The town meeting, which dates back to colonial days, is the most common form of town government in Rhode Island. Because voters participate directly in their government, town meetings have been called one of the purest forms of democracy. At town meetings, citizens elect officials, pass laws, and make decisions on other issues.

TAKE A TOUR OF PROVIDENCE, THE STATE CAPITAL

A statue of Roger Williams overlooks the city of Providence from Prospect Terrace.

The city of Providence has many identities. It became Rhode Island's official capital in 1900. Providence is a seaport and the largest city in the state, with a population of more than 173,000 people. It is also the chief manufacturing center of Rhode Island. The first town in the United States to allow freedom of religion, Providence is also a historical treasure.

State lawmakers meet in the Rhode Island State House. It is

made of white marble and has one of the only self-supporting marble domes in the world. On top of the dome is a gold-leaf statue called Independent Man, which overlooks the city. This statue reminds people that Rhode Island has always believed in freedom of religion and freedom of thought. Inside the State House is the original Rhode Island colony Charter of 1663.

A statue of "Independent Man" stands high atop the capitol's marble dome.

The Providence Arcade houses three floors of shops.

Southwest of downtown Providence is Roger Williams Park, named after the city's founder. It has the country's third oldest zoo, where more than 950 animals live. The park also includes a Museum of Natural History, which has a planetarium, displays about the people and wildlife of Narragansett Bay, and many Native American relics.

The Providence Arcade is the oldest indoor shopping mall in the United States. It is a lively place, especially at lunchtime, when the food courts sell everything from egg rolls to ice cream. Built in 1828, the Arcade is a National Landmark. A new mall, Providence Place, also provides plenty of indoor shopping opportunities.

One of the most popular tourist attractions is Benefit Street, nicknamed the Mile of History, on the east side of Providence.

Benefit Street is the heart of historic Providence.

Many beautifully restored colonial and Victorian houses, churches, and museums line Benefit Street or are within walking distance. The Providence Preservation Society conducts tours of the area.

The Museum of Art of the Rhode Island School of Design on Benefit Street is one of the finest small art museums in the country. It has more than 75,000 works, ranging from Greek bronzes to art from the Far East, to paintings by famous artists.

At Angell and North Main streets, the First Baptist Meeting House is open for worship. The nation's first Baptists worshiped there, led by Roger Williams, who founded the congregation in 1638. Baptists from all over the world look upon the First Baptist Meeting House as the "Mother Church."

West of Benefit Street on Hopkins Street is the Stephen Hopkins House. Hopkins, one of the founders of the nation, signed the Declaration of Independence and was governor of Rhode Island colony for ten terms. Many Early American buildings have signs boasting "George Washington slept here." The Stephen Hopkins House has a sign that says George Washington slept there—twice!

A few blocks from Benefit Street, the John Brown House, built in 1786, is a

WHO'S WHO IN RHODE ISLAND?

Edward Mitchell Bannister (1828–1901) was one of the few successful African-American artists of the nineteenth century. A landscape artist, he won the bronze medal in the 1876 Centennial in Philadelphia. Bannister completed more than one thousand paintings, some depicting scenes he sketched while sailing in his boat in Narragansett Bay. He co-founded the Providence Art Club and helped found the Rhode Island School of Design.

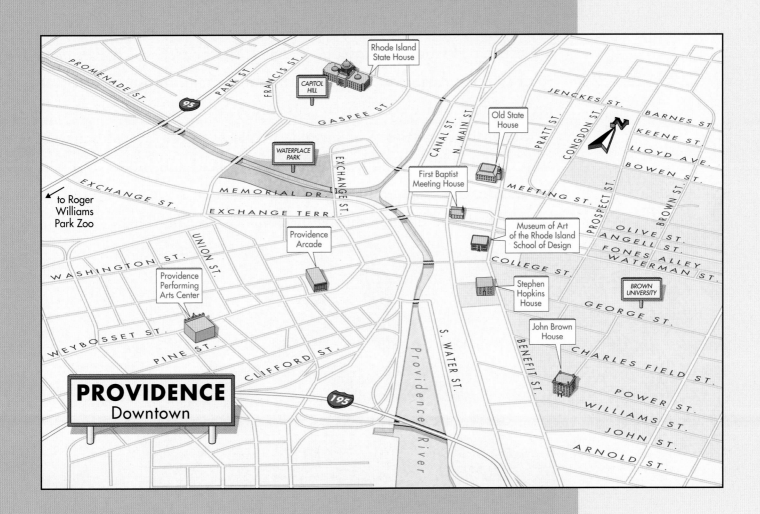

museum with beautiful eighteenth and nineteenth century furnishings. John Brown was one of four brothers of the wealthy Brown family of Providence. He wanted his house constructed where he could see the waterfront. His brother, Joseph, designed the house, which President John Quincy Adams once called "the most magnificent and elegant mansion that I have ever seen on this continent."

Brown University, one of the oldest colleges in the United States, is atop College Hill. Nicholas Brown provided land and money to build the college. Its oldest building, University Hall, served as a military headquarters and hospital during the American Revolution.

Visitors to the John Brown house can find out how a wealthy family lived in the 1700s.

CHAPTER FIVE

THE PEOPLE AND PLACES OF RHODE ISLAND

According to the 2000 Census, 1,048,319 people live in Rhode Island. It ranks forty-third in population among the states. Because of its small size, Rhode Island is the second most crowded, or densely populated, state. An average of 1,003 people live in 1 square mile (387 people per sq km) of land. (New Jersey is the most densely populated state.)

About 9 in 10 Rhode Islanders live in or near cities. Nearly two-thirds of the population is clustered in an industrial area along the north and west shores of the Narragansett Bay. Providence is Rhode Island's capital and one of the largest cities in New England. Pawtucket, War-wick, and Cranston are among the smaller cities nearby.

Nine in ten Rhode Islanders have European backgrounds, including English, Irish, Italian, French, and Portuguese. In recent years, many Hispanics have settled in the state. There are more than 90,000

Rhode Islanders honor their role in history through parades, reenactments, and other events.

A member of the Narragansett tribe, John "Great Wolf" Pompey, participates in a powwow in Charlestown.

Hispanics, mostly from Puerto Rico and the Dominican Republic. In addition, more than 45,000 African Americans and nearly 25,000 Asian Americans live in Rhode Island.

About 5,000 Native Americans live in Rhode Island today. Approximately 2,400 are Narragansett. Their tribal headquarters are in Charlestown. Narragansett culture and traditions flourish on the reservation. Tribal elders and youth can attend classes in Narragansett culture, history, and language on the reservation. There are many tribal celebrations open to the public, including the traditional August Meeting with music, dance, food, and storytelling.

WORKING IN RHODE ISLAND

Most of the people who are employed in Rhode Island—almost 8 in 10 workers—work in a service industry. A service industry is a business that provides a service for people or companies. A large part of Rhode Island's service industry includes jobs in finance, insurance, and real estate (the buying and selling of land, buildings, and homes.) Many New England banks have headquarters in Providence. The sale of goods is also important to the state's economy.

The government is another large employer in Rhode Island's service sector. Elected officials, judges, and medical staff in public hospitals work for the state of Rhode Island. The U.S. Navy facilities and the U.S. Naval War College employ many people. Teachers and school administrators are employed by public elementary and high schools, the University of Rhode Island, Rhode Island College, and the Community College of Rhode Island. Rhode Island educators also work in the state's many private colleges and universities, including Brown University, the Rhode Island School of Design, Roger Williams University, and Providence College.

The Navy has had a long history in Newport, thanks to its fine harbors and seaports.

Rhode Island was the birthplace of the American Industrial Revolution, and more than half of the state's workforce was employed in manufacturing during the late 1800s. A century later, jobs in manufacturing had declined, as they did in many states. Today, more than 80,000 Rhode Islanders are employed in the manufacturing industry.

Known as the Jewelry Capital of the world, Rhode Island produces more jewelry than any other state. Many jewelry manufacturers are located in the Providence area. Gorham Silver, founded in Providence in 1831 by Jabez Gorham, is one of the world's leading producers of sterling silver. Although Gorham is now owned by another company, it still

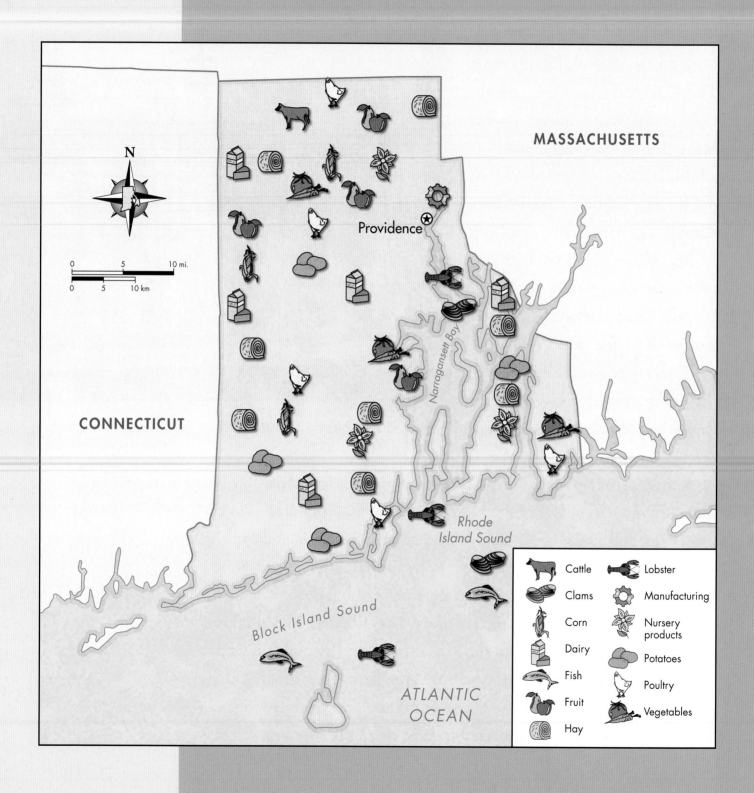

MASSACHUSETTS

CONNECTICUT

Providence

Narragansett Bay

Rhode
Island Sound

Block Island Sound

ATLANTIC
OCEAN

N

0   5   10 mi.

0   5   10 km

Cattle		Lobster	
Clams		Manufacturing	
Corn		Nursery products	
Dairy		Potatoes	
Fish		Poultry	
Fruit		Vegetables	
Hay			

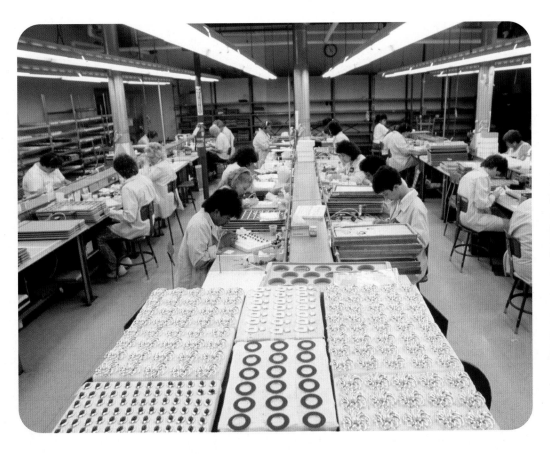

Employees in a Providence company produce great quantities of jewelry.

EXTRA! EXTRA!

The Rhode Island Red hen is prized for its ability to produce eggs. Each hen lays 200 to 300 eggs per year. The Rhode Island Red was developed by mating different kinds of hens in the mid-1800s. It became popular across the country because of its hardiness. Today, the original Rhode Island Red is rare. There are believed to be fewer than 2,500 in North America and fewer than 5,000 in the world.

employs workers in design and manufacturing in Smithfield. Other manufactured items include medical and scientific instruments, screws, nails, hand tools, electrical equipment, chemicals, plastics, specialty textiles such as lace and braid, and toys. Hasbro, Inc., a large toy manufacturer in Pawtucket, makes G.I. Joe® action figures, Mr. Potato Head®, and other toys. Yachts, boats, ships, and submarines are also manufactured in Rhode Island.

Agriculture, or farming, is only a small portion of Rhode Island's economy. About one tenth of the state's land is used for farming, with the best land along Narragansett Bay. Most of the state's farmers produce

More than half of Rhode Island's farms produce nursery products, such as ornamental shrubs shown here.

greenhouse and nursery products, such as Christmas trees and grass sod. Milk and other dairy products are the second leading agricultural products in the state. Chickens, turkeys, eggs, apples, potatoes, and hay are also produced in Rhode Island. The Rhode Island Red is a special breed of chicken developed in Little Compton, Rhode Island. It is the state bird.

The fishing industry in Rhode Island isn't as big as it used to be because there was too much fishing during the 1970s and 1980s. Pollution in Narragansett Bay also contributed to the decline of fishing.

Today, there are limits placed on commercial fishing, and the Narragansett Bay is being cleaned up. Lobsters, clams, cod, flounder, scup, squid, whiting, yellowfish, and many other species of fish are still plentiful.

TAKE A TOUR OF RHODE ISLAND

Northeastern Rhode Island

The largest cities in Rhode Island are located in the northeastern part of the state. It is the most crowded section of Rhode Island, with more than three-quarters of all Rhode Islanders living there. Providence, the state capital, is the largest city in Rhode Island.

Warwick is Rhode Island's second largest and fastest-growing city. Located on the western side of Narragansett Bay, it has a population of about 86,000. Warwick is the shopping capital of Rhode Island. Its "Miracle Mile of Shopping" has hundreds of shops and boutiques and two malls. The city is in the center of southern New England and near major highways, so it attracts shoppers from a large region. Warwick is nicknamed the "crossroads of southern New England."

West Warwick has a large Portuguese neighborhood. The Holy Ghost Festival is held every year on Labor Day weekend. People gather

Fishermen prepare to pull in the day's catch.

61

People of Portuguese descent in Rhode Island celebrate their heritage with traditional festivals and parades.

EXTRA! EXTRA!

Aldrich Mansion on Narragansett Bay in Warwick was the home of Nelson W. Aldrich, who served in the U.S. House of Representatives and the U.S. Senate. Born in poverty, Aldrich became wealthy in the grocery business and built a seventy-room mansion known as the Chateau. The home took sixteen years and nearly 200 craftspeople to build. Now open to the public, the mansion has wood carvings, Italian marble staircases and fireplaces, a music and fine arts chamber, and many valuable paintings. All of the windows have waist-high railings to protect Mrs. Aldrich, who had a habit of sleepwalking.

there to celebrate the Portuguese culture with traditional music, spicy chourico sandwiches, barbecued beef, and Portuguese sweet bread.

Cranston, Rhode Island's third largest city, was part of Providence until 1727. Just south of Providence, Cranston now has a population of almost 80,000. The Governor Sprague Mansion in Cranston is a popular tourist attraction. It is a beautifully restored home built in the 1790s. It was once the home of two Rhode Island governors—William Sprague and his nephew of the same name. Visitors can tour the house and the carriage house, which contains sleighs, carriages, a pony cart, and a gypsy wagon.

The annual Gaspee Days celebration takes place in Warwick and Cranston from mid-May to June. It commemorates the burning of the British schooner *Gaspee* by Rhode Island patriots in 1772. There is an arts and crafts fair, a children's colonial costume contest, and a weekend camp-out in which campers wear colonial era clothes and re-enact life during the American Revolution. At the end of the festivities, a symbolic burning of the *Gaspee* takes place in the waters of Pawtuxet Cove.

The city of Newport is south of Providence, on a peninsula off the southern tip of Aquidneck Island. Newport attracts tourists from all over the world. The lavish mansions built by the wealthy in the early 1900s are one of the town's most popular attractions. Many of the homes are owned by the Preservation Society of Newport County and are open to the public. Visitors enjoy hiking the Cliff Walk, a 3-mile (5-km) path along the ocean that runs parallel to the mansion-lined streets.

Built in 1893, the Breakers is one of Newport's grandest mansions, with 70 rooms inside.

History buffs love the many landmarks in Newport's historic district near the waterfront. The Colony House in Washington Square was once one of Rhode Island's two state capitols. Many shops and restaurants line the square's old Brick Market.

Sailing, tennis, and music are also big in Newport. The seaside

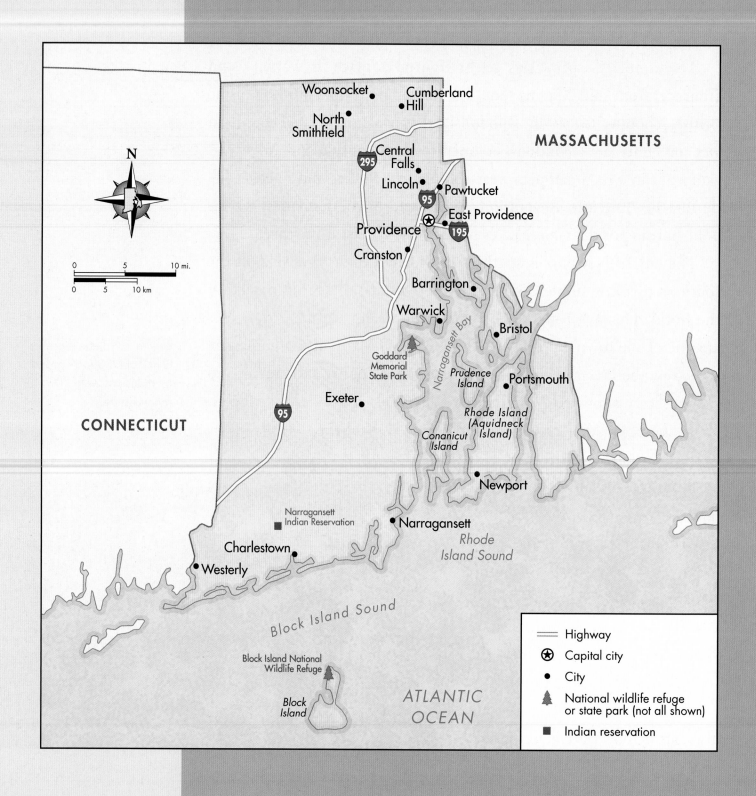

Woonsocket

Cumberland
Hill

North
Smithfield

Central
Falls

295

Lincoln

Pawtucket

95

East Providence

195

Providence

Cranston

Barrington

Warwick

Bristol

Goddard
Memorial
State Park

Narragansett Bay

Prudence
Island

Portsmouth

95

Exeter

Rhode Island
(Aquidneck
Island)

Conanicut
Island

Newport

Narragansett
Indian Reservation

Narragansett

Rhode
Island Sound

Charlestown

Westerly

MASSACHUSETTS

CONNECTICUT

N

0   5   10 mi.

0   5   10 km

Block Island Sound

Block Island National
Wildlife Refuge

Block
Island

ATLANTIC
OCEAN

══	Highway
✪	Capital city
●	City
🌲	National wildlife refuge or state park (not all shown)
■	Indian reservation

In colonial days, Rhode Islanders often made these pancakes out of cornmeal and ate them hot or cold with maple syrup. The name may have originally been "journey-cakes" because they were easy to make on long trips. Don't forget to ask an adult for help!

JOHNNYCAKES

> 1-1/2 cups cornmeal
> 1 egg
> 1/2 cup milk
> 1/4 teaspoon salt

1. Mix all ingredients together in a large bowl. Add more milk if too dry. The batter should be thick but not runny.
2. Grease a griddle or frying pan and preheat.
3. Drop spoonfuls of batter on griddle or frying pan. Fry until crisp. Turn and fry the other side until done.
4. Serve hot with butter and/or syrup.

Green Animals is one of the most well-known gardens of its kind in the country.

town hosts many world-famous sailing races. The Museum of Yachting is located in Fort Adams State Park. The Campbell's Hall of Fame Tennis Championships are held in Newport, where visitors can also tour the International Tennis Hall of Fame. Established in 1954, the annual Newport Jazz Festival has featured some of the finest jazz artists in the world, such as Dizzy Gillespie, Ella Fitzgerald, and Billie Holiday.

On the outskirts of Newport, the Green Animals of Portsmouth are an unusual attraction. The "animals" are topiaries, or sculptured hedges. You can see the likenesses of animals such as elephants, camels, boars, giraffes, and peacocks there.

South County

The lower third of Rhode Island's mainland is Washington County, but many refer to it as South County. The region is dotted with quaint fishing villages, beaches, forests, wildlife refuges, and ponds. The tribal headquarters of the Narragansett, known as the Long House, is in Charlestown. The state turned over the land to the Narragansett in 1983. The tribe holds its annual meeting there in August with dancing, singing, crafts, and traditional foods and games. Tribe members teach classes on Narragansett culture, history, and language. There is also a community garden.

With 11 miles (18 km) of coastline, the town of Narragansett has most of the state beaches. The University of Rhode Island's School of Oceanography is at its north end. Fishing fleets launch from Galilee at Narragansett's southern tip. From there, visitors can take a ferry to Block Island and enjoy its rugged cliffs, sandy beaches, and cozy inns. The small, quiet island is perfect for biking, hiking, kayaking, and canoeing. Bird lovers especially enjoy the island, because songbirds stop there on the way south in the fall. The Block Island National Wildlife Refuge of sand dunes and beaches is a haven for gulls.

Water Street on Block Island offers shops, restaurants, and the perfect setting for bicyclists.

Pawtucket and the Blackstone Valley

Rhode Island's fourth largest city has a population of about 73,000. Located on the Blackstone River, Pawtucket is known as "the cradle of American industry." Early industrialists harnessed the power of the waterfalls to run mills and factories. Slater Mill Historic Site has two mills, a theater, and a gallery. Samuel Slater built the country's first

Baseball fans cheer on the Pawtucket Red Sox (the PawSox) at McCoy Stadium.

water-powered mill there. Visitors can see demonstrations of how machines turn raw cotton into thread and then knit them into clothing such as T-shirts. Pawtucket is also the site of McCoy Stadium, home of the PawSox, an AAA affiliate of the Boston Red Sox.

Central Falls, Woonsocket, Lincoln, Cumberland, and North Smithfield are also nestled along the Blackstone River. Many of the mills in these towns have been converted to museums. Unfortunately, some are empty and in disrepair. Central Falls has the state's second largest Puerto Rican population. Its annual Fiesta de Pueblo celebrates Puerto Rican music, poetry, and dance. Visitors to the Blackstone Valley also enjoy canoeing and touring wildlife preserves.

Inland Rhode Island

The peace and quiet of rural communities make up inland Rhode Island. Farms, rivers, ponds, and wildlife refuges can be found in this part of the state. The Arcadia Management Area, with more than 13,800 acres (5,585 ha) is filled with pine forests, wildflowers, and hiking trails. Sightseers stop at farmers' markets during summer and fall to buy corn, peaches, pumpkins, baked goods, jams, and jellies.

RHODE ISLAND ALMANAC

Official state name: State of Rhode Island and Providence Plantations

Statehood date and number: May 29, 1790; 13th state

State seal: The seal features a golden anchor with the word "Hope" above it. The phrase "Seal of the State of Rhode Island and Providence Plantations 1636" surrounds the anchor. Adopted in 1896.

State flag: The flag features a golden anchor on a white background. A blue ribbon with the word "Hope" is under the anchor. Thirteen gold stars form a circle around the anchor and the ribbon. Adopted in 1897.

Geographic center: Kent, 1 mile (2 km) south-south-west of Crompton

Total area/rank: 1,545 square miles (4,002 sq km)/50th

Coastline: More than 400 miles (644 km)

Borders: Massachusetts, Connecticut, Atlantic Ocean

Latitude and longitude: Rhode Island is located at approximately 41.8° N and 71.4° W

Highest/lowest elevation: 812 feet (247 m) above sea level, Jerimoth Hill in the northwest/sea level along the Atlantic Ocean

Hottest/coldest temperature: 104° F (40° C) on August 2, 1975, in Providence/–25° F (–32° C) on February 5, 1996, at Greene

Total land area/rank: 1,045 square miles (2,706 sq km)/50th

Inland water area/rank: 178 square miles (461 sq km)/46th

Population/rank: 1,048,319 (2000 Census)/43rd

Population of major cities:

Providence: 173,618

Warwick: 85,808

Cranston: 79,269

Pawtucket: 72,958

East Providence: 48,688

Origin of state name: Some say Giovanni da Verrazzano thought a nearby island looked like the island of Rhodes near Greece; others say Adriaen Block named a nearby island *Roodt Eylandt*—Dutch words meaning "red island"—after the island's red clay soil.

State capital: Providence

Previous capitals: Five capitals from 1663 to 1854. Newport and Providence were co-capitals from 1854 to 1900.

Number of counties: 5

State government: 38 senators, 75 representatives

Major rivers/lakes: Pawtucket, Blackstone, Seekonk, Providence, Moshassuck, Woonasquatucket, Pawcatuck/Scituate Reservoir, Watchaug Pond, Ninigret Pond, Quonochontaug Pond, Point Judith Pond

Farm products: Turf, greenhouse and nursery products, dairy, potatoes, hay, apples, berries, corn

Livestock: Poultry, dairy cows, hogs

Manufactured products: Jewelry, silverware, metal products, scientific instruments, ships, plastics

Mining products: Gravel, stone, sand

Fishing products: Lobster, clams, squid, bass, eels, perch, pickerel, trout, bluefish, flounder, swordfish, tuna

Bird: Rhode Island Red hen

Colors: Blue, white, and gold

Flower: Violet

Mineral: Bowenite

Motto: Hope

Nicknames: The Ocean State, Little Rhody

Shell: Quahaug

Song: "Rhode Island It's For Me," lyrics by Charlie Hall, music by Maria Day

Stone: Cumberlandite

Tree: Red maple

Wildlife: Deer, foxes, minks, muskrats, otters, rabbits, raccoons, squirrels, owls, robins, blue jays, loons, ospreys, gulls, ducks, partridges, peasants

TIMELINE

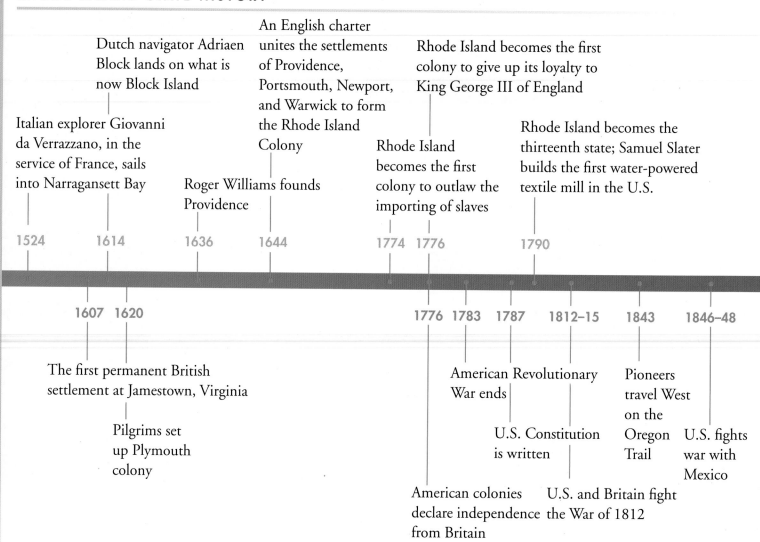

Italian explorer Giovanni da Verrazzano, in the service of France, sails into Narragansett Bay

Dutch navigator Adriaen Block lands on what is now Block Island

Roger Williams founds Providence

An English charter unites the settlements of Providence, Portsmouth, Newport, and Warwick to form the Rhode Island Colony

Rhode Island becomes the first colony to outlaw the importing of slaves

Rhode Island becomes the first colony to give up its loyalty to King George III of England

Rhode Island becomes the thirteenth state; Samuel Slater builds the first water-powered textile mill in the U.S.

1524   1614   1636   1644   1774 1776   1790

1607 1620   1776 1783 1787   1812–15   1843   1846–48

The first permanent British settlement at Jamestown, Virginia

Pilgrims set up Plymouth colony

American Revolutionary War ends

U.S. Constitution is written

American colonies declare independence from Britain

U.S. and Britain fight the War of 1812

Pioneers travel West on the Oregon Trail

U.S. fights war with Mexico

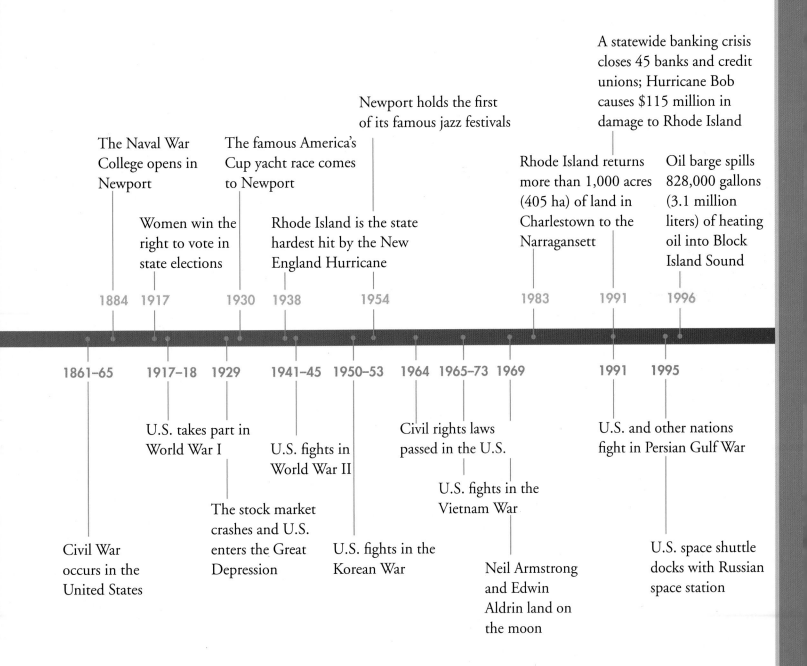

A statewide banking crisis closes 45 banks and credit unions; Hurricane Bob causes $115 million in damage to Rhode Island

Newport holds the first of its famous jazz festivals

The Naval War College opens in Newport

The famous America's Cup yacht race comes to Newport

Rhode Island returns more than 1,000 acres (405 ha) of land in Charlestown to the Narragansett

Oil barge spills 828,000 gallons (3.1 million liters) of heating oil into Block Island Sound

Women win the right to vote in state elections

Rhode Island is the state hardest hit by the New England Hurricane

1884   1917   1930   1938   1954   1983   1991   1996

1861–65   1917–18   1929   1941–45   1950–53   1964   1965–73   1969   1991   1995

U.S. takes part in World War I

U.S. fights in World War II

Civil rights laws passed in the U.S.

U.S. and other nations fight in Persian Gulf War

U.S. fights in the Vietnam War

The stock market crashes and U.S. enters the Great Depression

U.S. fights in the Korean War

Civil War occurs in the United States

Neil Armstrong and Edwin Aldrin land on the moon

U.S. space shuttle docks with Russian space station

GALLERY OF FAMOUS RHODE ISLANDERS

George M. Cohan
(1878–1942)
Composer, musician, actor, and playwright. He is known as the father of U.S. musical comedy. Cohan wrote more than five hundred songs, including "Yankee Doodle Dandy." Born in Providence.

Leon N. Cooper
(1930–)
Physicist who taught and conducted research related to electricity and electrons at Brown University. Cooper won the 1972 Nobel Prize in physics with two other scientists. He is a senior professor at Brown.

Sissieretta Jones
(1869–1933)
One of the most famous African-American singers in America. Jones sang for U.S. presidents and European royalty and won many medals for her talent. Longtime resident of Providence.

Irving Raskin Levine
(1922–)
Respected broadcast journalist. He was a reporter for the NBC television network for more than thirty-five years. Born in Pawtucket.

Ida Lewis
(1842–1911)
Lighthouse keeper known as the Heroine of Lime Rock. She helped save the lives of many sailors during the 1800s. Born in Newport.

H. P. Lovecraft
(1890–1937)
Author of science fiction and horror books; he included many Providence landmarks in his stories. Lovecraft was so devoted to Providence that his gravestone reads "I am Providence." Born in Providence.

Gilbert Stuart
(1755–1828)
One of the most gifted American portrait painters of his time. He painted a number of portraits of George Washington, including the one that appears on the dollar bill. Born in Saunderstown.

Chris Van Allsburg
(1949–)
Award-winning writer and illustrator of children's books, including *Jumanji* and *The Polar Express*. Teaches illustration at Rhode Island School of Design.

GLOSSARY

amendment: a change to a constitution

charter: written grant of rights

colony: part of a new country where a large group of people move, who are still ruled by the leaders and laws of their old country

constitution: laws and principles a government is based upon

democracy: government by the people, usually through elected representatives

glacier: a large mass of ice and snow

home rule: cities and towns that are permitted to write and change their charters without permission from the legislature

immigrant: person who comes to a new country or region to settle there

legislators: lawmakers

longhouse: long, narrow Native American dwelling framed with logs covered in bark

majority: more than half of a total, such as more than half the votes in favor of a candidate or bill

Protestants: Christians who are not Roman Catholic or Eastern Orthodox

Puritans: people in the 1500s and 1600s who belonged to the Protestant branch of the Christian church

Quakers: Christian group against violence that refused to take an oath of loyalty to the king of England or the Puritan Church

reservoir: an artificial lake where a large amount of water is stored for purposes of irrigation, hydroelectric power, etc.

strike: when workers refuse to continue working until certain demands are met, such as higher pay or better working conditions

synagogue: place of worship for those of the Jewish faith

taxes: a portion of a citizen's wages or the value of a good or service that is paid to support the government

textiles: fabric or cloth made by weaving or knitting

town meeting: form of democracy in which voters participate directly in their government

FOR MORE INFORMATION

Web Sites

Rhode Island Tourism

www.VisitRhodeIsland.com

Information on places to visit and stay in Rhode Island, as well as information about state history and geography.

Governor of Rhode Island

www.gov.state.ri.us

Web site for the governor of Rhode Island, with links to events, speeches, data about Rhode Island, and the U.S. Census.

Rhode Island Office of the Secretary of State

www.state.ri.us

Official Web site for the Rhode Island Secretary of State, with links to Rhode Island officials and the General Assembly, the State Library, and Rhode Island tourism.

The U.S.50, Inc.

www.theus50.com/rhodeisland

Information about Rhode Island, including history, geography, and travel.

The Narragansett Tribe

www.narragansett-tribe.org.

Information about the history and culture of the Narragansett tribe.

Books

Howarth, Sarah. *Colonial People.* Brookfield, CT: The Millbrook Press, 1994.

Howarth, Sarah. *Colonial Places.* Brookfield, CT: The Millbrook Press, 1994.

McCurdy, Michael. *The Year According to the Fall Moon.* Boston: Houghton Mifflin, 2000.

Rappaport, Doreen. *Escape from Slavery: Five Journeys to Freedom.* New York: HarperCollins, 1991.

Waters, Kate. *Tapenum's Day: a Wampanoag Indian Boy in Pilgrim Times.* New York: Scholastic, 1996.

Whitehurst, Susan. *The Colony of Rhode Island.* New York: Rosen Publishing Group, 2000.

Addresses

Rhode Island Tourism Division

315 Iron Horse Way, Suite 101
Providence, RI 02908

Narragansett Indian Tribe

P. O. Box 268
Charlestown, RI 02813

INDEX